Long-Term Community Recovery Planning Process

A Guide to Determining Project Recovery Values

February 2006

This DRAFT version of the Long-Term Community Recovery (LTCR) Recovery Value Tool presents a standardized methodology for determining the recovery value of post-disaster reconstruction projects. Prioritizing need, identifying projects to meet the need and determining which projects have the highest recovery value are critical steps to guide a community's long-term recovery from a disaster. The Tool incorporates best practices developed on a number of successful pilot recovery planning initiatives throughout the country. The Tool has been released with expedited review and is intended to meet the immediate needs of the communities impacted by the 2005 hurricane season. It is expected that revisions will be made to this tool as a result of refinement of the Long-Term Community Recovery planning process.

Table of Contents

INTRODUCTION

Communities face many challenges following a disaster, including determining where the limited resources for their recovery are to be expended. After the initial "emergency" phase of a disaster response is completed, such as the rescue of those in need, the repair of critical services including water and power, and the restoration of key governmental functions, a community becomes focused on its long-term rebuilding.

It is important to understand that there may be multiple funding sources available after a disaster event, but that resources may not be sufficient to undertake all the projects a community may ultimately need for full recovery. A first step for many communities may be to look to existing local comprehensive plans, capital improvement plans, hazard mitigation plans, or other similar documents to identify previously developed project priorities.

The process identified in this Recovery Value Tool builds upon those priorities and provides a systematic methodology to evaluate recovery projects for the community. Fundamentally, this tool allows for an evaluation of priorities based upon the impacts of the recent disaster and the physical and community needs that have been caused by the event. Therefore, this process can provide a comprehensive evaluation of the needs, identify the most effective projects for the resources available, and allow for a more holistic combination of resources to accomplish the community's goals.

Background

During a community's recovery period a number of federal programs are implemented that serve to aid in the rebuilding and hardening of a community. These include, among others, FEMA's Public Assistance and Hazard Mitigation Grant Programs, as well as the Department of Housing and Urban Development's (HUD) Community Development Block Grant (CDBG) Program. The National Response Plan establishes Emergency Support Function (ESF)14, Long-Term Community Recovery, to coordinate federal technical assistance for community recovery planning and federal resources for implementing community recovery projects. The Recovery Value Tool may be used by ESF 14 agencies to assist communities during long term community recovery planning, or after smaller disaster events when ESF 14 is not activated, it may be used by FEMA for the same purpose.

This Recovery Value Tool:
- ⊙ Is intended to assist a long-term community recovery planning team in assessing the recovery value of projects derived from the planning process and to eventually assign specific Recovery Values to projects that are contained in the community's recovery plan;

- Addresses the recovery process in a comprehensive manner and takes a holistic perspective on the process of determining a project's value to the recovery of a particular community;
- Provides a summary of the recovery value concept that can be used in each community recovery plan as an explanation to federal, state, and local agencies as well as to the community in general.

Objectives and Use of the Recovery Value Tool

The objective of the Recovery Value Tool is to assist in determining a project's value to the long-term recovery of a community from a particular disaster. The Recovery Value Tool will:

- Define what a Recovery Value is and how it fits into the planning process
- Provide an objective assessment of each project's recovery value
- Assist in determining implementation priorities
- Provide documentation to funding agencies regarding a project's anticipated long-term impact

The Recovery Value Tool (Tool) is designed for use by FEMA or other agencies to provide technical assistance to communities during long-term recovery planning. The spreadsheet-based Recovery Value Tool can be used to provide FEMA, other federal and state agencies, and the local community with an assessment of a project's potential impact on the long-term recovery of a community. The Tool includes criteria and measurement of a project's value to the long-term recovery effort, a summary of the recovery value concept that can be used in LTCR plans and documents, and a graphic and visual means of conveying each project's recovery value. This will assist in determining project timing, funding priorities, and overall management of the long-term recovery process.

DEFINITION OF PROJECT RECOVERY VALUE

Experience in past FEMA LTCR initiatives has shown that projects identified during the planning process have varying levels of impact on the recovery of a community. The purpose of this Tool is to provide general guidance to communities and recovery personnel as to the characteristics that typically make some projects more beneficial to recovery than others. The Tool does not attempt to evaluate the overall importance of any project to the community – only to the process of recovering from disasters of all types.

Recovery Value is the designation assigned to a project that indicates its ability to help jump-start a community's recovery from a natural disaster or incident of national significance. Projects that positively contribute to recovery typically address a broad range of issues that promote a functioning and healthy economy, support infrastructure optimization, and encourage provision of a full range of housing opportunities.

Each project in a LTCR Plan will be assigned one of three Recovery Values: High, Moderate, and Low. A fourth category, "Community Interest", will be used to designate projects that have significant local support, but either cannot be implemented in a timeframe that will substantively affect recovery, or do not clearly promote any key disaster recovery goals.

The value attached to each project is based on the degree to which it assists the community in its recovery from a disaster, and is predicated on a series of general criteria:
- Meets a Post-Disaster Community Need
- Is Sustainable
- Is Feasible
- Provides Benefits that Cut Across Several Areas in the Community ("Cross-cutting Benefits")
    - Stimulates the Economy
    - Has High Visibility
    - Provides Linkages
    - Contributes to the Community's Quality of Life

High Recovery Value Project

Those projects assigned a high recovery value are catalyst projects that have multiple impacts on the community and its recovery. Typically, a High Recovery Value project will:
- Be directly related to damages
- Have community support and community-wide benefits
- Be achievable (within a 3-5 year recovery timeline) and sustainable
- Have a champion
- Incorporate identified best practices for reducing loss in the future
- Create economic opportunities

o Have a high visibility and build community capacity
o Leverage and create linkages to other projects and resources
o Enhance quality of life for the community

Moderate Recovery Value Project

A moderate recovery value project is limited in scope, span, impact or benefits. It will:
o Have limited community support and benefits
o Include a limited amount of identified best practices for reducing future losses
o Have less definable outcomes
o Provide benefits for some economic sectors
o Leverage and create linkages to other projects and resources
o Enhance quality of life for the community

Low Recovery Value Project

Low Recovery Value projects:
o May have an indirect link to the disaster and its damages
o Have little community support or benefits
o Lack the necessary resources
o Are difficult to achieve or sustain

Community Interest Project

A Community Interest project does not have a significant recovery value, but it:
o May be extremely important to a community
o Addresses a long-standing community interest
o Has significant public support
o May not produce results within 3-5 year recovery timeline
o May emerge from long-standing plans that have never been implemented
o Has no relationship to the disaster
o Does not produce identifiable benefits that promote recovery

An example of a Community Interest Project might be the memorial to the victims of the tornado in Utica, Illinois. While the project itself did not contribute to the physical or economic recovery of the community, it had significant community support and contributed to the emotional recovery of the residents.

PROJECT RECOVERY VALUE METHODOLOGY AND PROCESS

The Recovery Value Tool enables FEMA, other federal and state agencies, the affected community, and the Long-Term Community Recovery Planning Team to determine which recovery projects are likely to have the most significant impact on recovery of the affected area. The Tool is intended to be used by the Long-Term Community Recovery Planning Team as they develop projects in support of the long-term recovery process. The Tool allows the Planning Team to provide better information to FEMA and potential funding agencies, and allows the affected community to focus resources on projects most likely to promote substantive recovery from a disaster.

How are Projects Generated?

The responsibility for recommending projects for a community's long-term recovery plan rests with the Long-Term Community Recovery Planning Team. Members of the planning team typically have experience in comprehensive planning, design, engineering, and capital improvements. That experience, coupled with the community involvement process (where issues and potential projects have been discussed) and the FEMA Public Assistance and Mitigation activities, form the basis for generation of projects. Collectively, the projects identified should accomplish the vision and goals identified in the first weeks of the LTCR process. But the focus of the planning team should be on projects that have the greatest impact on the long-term recovery of the community. Determining the recovery value of each project provides guidance for community decision-makers as they implement the plan and assists in determining funding priorities.

The various components of a project have an impact on its recovery value. *A checklist, or series of questions for project development, is contained in Appendix III*. These items are ultimately related to the criteria used in determining the recovery value of a project. Referencing this list and incorporating some of the elements as a project is being generated may ultimately result in a project that has a greater impact on the community's long-term recovery.

Recovery Value Tool Methodology

The Recovery Value Tool has been developed by planners, designers, and social scientists with extensive experience in long-term community recovery planning. The basic methodology employed to determine the recovery value of a project consists of assessing a number of criteria relating to the damage from the disaster and the particular nature and attributes of the project. Some criteria focus on the type, location, and extent of the damage and how the project addresses that damage. Other criteria focus on specific attributes of the project in terms of its feasibility, sustainability, economic impact, linkage with other projects, etc.

The criteria used in the Tool were chosen based on Long-Term Community Recovery efforts undertaken over the past several years and the key recovery projects that evolved from those efforts. While it is too early in the implementation phase to adequately measure the ultimate recovery value of these projects, their impacts have been studied and the individual projects have been analyzed to determine their key attributes.

The Recovery Value Tool assesses how each project measures up to the various criteria. Projects that are multi-dimensional and comprehensive in nature generally have the highest recovery value. This Tool provides a systematic and consistent process for determination of a project's recovery value for a community.

Validation of Tool

The Recovery Value Tool has been applied to projects contained in previous LTCR planning efforts to determine its validity. Criteria were modified, deleted, and added as a result of this process. While the Recovery Value Tool should be viewed as a working document subject to review and revisions based on application experience, testing on actual LTCR projects has validated the Tool and its underlying assumptions.

Tool as a Guide

The Recovery Value Tool serves as a guide in determining a project's value for a community's recovery. Results of the Tool should play an important role as the long-term recovery professional assesses a project's impact on recovery; however, the Tool is not meant to be formulaic and, therefore, the "score" should not be the sole determinant of a project's recovery value. The long-term recovery team should use the Tool and the professional experience of its members in determining a project's overall recovery value. For example, a housing development project proposed for a neighborhood adjacent to downtown may not score enough points to be designated a High Recovery Value Project, but the planning team knows that the impact of the project on a neighborhood and downtown that received extensive damage will be significant and could generate other future projects. The planning team should identify such a project as High Recovery Value.

It should be emphasized that the Recovery Value Tool is a GUIDE for the planning team. The professional judgment and expertise of the planning team and the unique aspects of each community are important in assigning recovery value to each project.

Use of the Tool

It is recommended that all members of the planning team be involved in determining each project's recovery value. Typically each member of the planning team will have responsibility for developing one or more projects for the LTCR plan. Each planning team member should use the recovery value Tool to assess the value of his or her project. Upon completion of the assessment, the team member should recommend an appropriate recovery value for their project and forward their recommendation and the results of the Tool to the planning team leader.

The designation of each project's recovery value is the responsibility of the planning team leader; however, input from the team members most closely involved with project development is important. Upon receipt of the recovery value assessments for all projects, the team leader should convene a meeting of all team members to review each project and its recovery value. The intent of this planning team discussion is to arrive at a general consensus on the recovery values of all projects contained in the community's recovery plan. Although this review is important, the ultimate responsibility for designation of project recovery value lies with the planning team leader.

Categories

The Recovery Value tool is comprised of three primary recovery categories and one general category. The general category captures overall benefits of the project across several aspects of the community. The categories are:

1. Post-Disaster Community Need
2. Project Feasibility
3. Project Sustainability
4. Cross-cutting Benefits
   a. Stimulates the Economy
   b. Has High Visibility
   c. Provides Linkages
   d. Contributes to the Community's Quality of Life

A description of each of these categories and the factors and criteria used to assess a project are presented in the following pages. A detailed spreadsheet is included in the Rating System section that addresses each of the Categories, the various Factors and Criteria used, Guidance Notes for Scoring, and a Rating System. The Rating System spreadsheets contain:

- The specific criteria and information needed to assess each factor
- The source and location of that information (if needed)
- Guidance notes for rating each criteria and factor

- A score for each criteria
- Overall score that identifies the project's value in the community's recovery from the disaster

Scoring

The scoring for the Tool employs a scale and requires professional judgment. Each criterion receives a score based on the degree to which the project meets the indicated factors that serve as a scoring guide. Determination of the score for particular criteria may require interpretation and subjectivity. That cannot be avoided; however, the Tool is formulated to provide an objective assessment of what are sometimes subjective interpretations.

Suggested scoring on a scale from 1 to 3

1 = **Low** match w/ criteria

2 = **Moderate** match w/ criteria

3 = **High** match w/ criteria

High Recovery Value
A High Recovery Value score results when the following occurs:
- A project scores an average of 2.5 or higher

Moderate Recovery Value
A Moderate Recovery Value score results when the following occurs:
- A project scores an average of 1.5 to 2.4

Low Recovery Value
A Low Recovery Value score results when the following occurs:
- A project scores an average of 1.4 or less

Community Interest
A Community Interest score results when a project obtains a low recovery value designation but there is strong community support for the project. These projects generally cannot be implemented in a timeframe to affect recovery or may not clearly promote key disaster recovery goals.

> *The above score ranges for Low, Moderate, and High are guides. The ranges may need to be modified for different communities. The key is to use the Tool as a guide and apply professional judgment in conjunction with the results of the RV Tool.*

The following sections provide a description of the three primary categories and the cross-cutting benefits category.

Post-Disaster Community Need

The Project...

Meets a Post-Disaster Community Need

When a disaster strikes it impacts a community in a variety of ways – no two communities are alike, each has different needs in response to a disaster. These needs have a significant impact on the response to a disaster and on a community's recovery. Community Need varies depending upon the magnitude of the event and the impact of damages affecting the community. Identifying the issues and prioritizing the needs allows each community to control the recovery process.

The Tool provides a framework to evaluate how a project supports a "community need" as a result of a disaster. The Post-Disaster Community Need of project is measured based on the following criteria:

Direct Damages
- <u>Damage</u> – project received direct damage from the disaster and is a catalyst for community recovery.
- <u>Improvement</u> – project provides an opportunity to improve upon pre-disaster conditions – especially with regard to projects eligible for FEMA Public Assistance.

Fills a Gap
- <u>Planned</u> – project addresses an issue or need that has been previously identified in other community plans or documents or is validated by or attained new urgency from the disaster.
- <u>Essential</u> – includes projects that are necessary to the health and safety of the community.

Leverage
- <u>Funding</u> – the project leverages several sources of funding.

Community Support and Impact
- <u>Support</u> – includes projects that have documented community support; i.e., tangible broad-based support, not just one special interest with an agenda.
- <u>Households</u> – includes projects that primarily benefit low to moderate income households.
- <u>Social and Cultural Impact</u> – projects that address or support distinct social or cultural attributes.

Feasibility

The Project...

Meets Project Feasibility Criteria

A post-disaster recovery project that is considered important to a community may satisfy a number of important criteria that suggest it should be pursued. But one of the most critical factors determining whether a project is worth undertaking is also a matter of practicality: How feasible is it? Can the project actually be achieved with available resources, within regulatory and logistical constraints, and within a realistic timeframe? Does it have sufficient community support to get off the ground?

This Tool provides a framework for evaluating how "feasible" a project is based on whether it meets the following criteria:

Builds Upon Available Resources
- All Necessary Resources – project meets the criteria of and has access to sources of funding—local, state, federal, foundation, private donor, and other—necessary to cover *a significant portion of* project costs within project timeframe. Project also has access to a majority of other necessary resources such as volunteers, donations of other goods and services, and other tangible resources necessary for the project. NOTE: Though special federal and/or state appropriations may be available, they should not be relied upon in assessing the feasibility of a project *unless* final formal commitments have been made.

Conforms to Regulatory, Logistical, and Planning Constraints
- Compatible with Government Initiatives and Local Planning – not in conflict with other local, state, and federal initiatives undertaken for recovery or community development; supports and enhances other initiative activities and/or local planning activities.
- Compatible with Other Regulatory Constraints – not in conflict with existing statutes or regulations.

Is Achievable
- Definable Outcomes – project scope is clearly defined in terms of achievability; measurable outcomes take into account concept-level costs.
- Workable Timeframe – the project can be completed within a reasonable and practical timeframe that is responsive to community need, that is compatible with other planning efforts (especially if those efforts rely on this project's completion), and that can be achieved within the limits of available resources.

- ⏱ <u>Other Characteristics Affecting Project Feasibility</u> – might include design or plan flexibility, ease of implementation, identification of a sufficient range of options that will increase the likelihood of project success, etc. Generally, a cost/benefit assessment is not necessary but one may be required for those projects that demonstrate community interest but are questionable as to the feasibility for funding and implementation.

Has a Champion
- ⏱ <u>Identified, Committed Champion</u> – a local individual or group with sufficient enthusiasm, time, political influence, and access to resources to complete the project.

Sustainable Development

The Project...

Meets LTCR Sustainable Development Criteria

The most common and persistent sustainability issue that local communities face during LTCR is the development of financially sustainable projects that will pay for themselves or those that local governments can afford over time. In addition to this factor, those projects that help prevent acts of nature from becoming disasters, as well as those that advance resource conservation and efficiency, define sustainable development in the unique context of LTCR. Examples of sustainable development include hazard mitigation projects such as relocating a structure, restricting new construction in particularly vulnerable areas, elevating structures to remove the threat of flooding, or building smarter, stronger buildings and utilities that are more hazard-resistant.

It also includes projects that promote resource efficiency, or the prudent use of energy, water, and natural resources to ensure healthy communities for future generations to come. Whether recovery means putting damaged homes and communities back together or building new ones, the process creates numerous opportunities for incorporating forward-thinking, sustainable technologies. For example, energy efficient technologies can be incorporated into new or renovated buildings; the site design for new communities and neighborhoods can take into account the natural topography and accommodate efficient modes of transportation; and new infrastructure can include local renewable resources and innovative wastewater treatment technologies. These types of projects enable disaster-prone communities to become active drivers toward change, rather than passive victims of nature.

The Tool provides a framework for evaluating how "sustainable" a project is based on whether it meets the following criteria:

Financially Sustainable
- Affordable over the Long-Term – construction and/or operation estimates of the project demonstrate that the project would pay for itself or can be financed by the local government without additional aid over the long-term.

Averts Future Losses
- Planned Mitigation – includes previously planned hazard mitigation or safety and security measures as identified in existing federal, state, or local plans.
- Applies Mitigation Measures – project applies a mitigation or safety measure to avert future losses (planned and/or unplanned).

Uses Built and Natural Resources Efficiently

- ⏱ <u>Land Use</u> – advances the efficient use of land; limits urban sprawl; advances Brownfield, greyfield, and infill development; decreases impervious surfaces; promotes mixed use and mixed income neighborhoods; and / or promotes other smart growth principles.
- ⏱ <u>Connectivity</u> – geographically located to encourage safe, convenient, and efficient connectivity with other nodes of development within the community.
- ⏱ <u>Natural Environment Protection</u> – protects or restores key ecosystems; protects wildlife and natural areas; and / or improves water and air quality.
- ⏱ <u>Water and Energy Use Reduction</u> – assessed by estimating the reduction in water and energy use; can include innovative wastewater technologies.
- ⏱ <u>Transportation</u> – improves availability of mass transit or advances multiple transportation solutions for those who need it.

Cross-Cutting Benefits

A project's Cross-Cutting Benefit is measured based on the following criteria, which are further defined and detailed in the discussions for each category.

- Impact on the economy and economic sector of the community
    - Getting people back to work
    - Sustaining existing businesses and attracting new ones
    - Creating new economic opportunities
- High visibility and ability to build community capacity
    - Community investment
    - Awareness
    - Catalyst projects
    - Multiple benefits
    - Visionary
- Ability to provide linkages throughout the community and connections to other projects and funding resources
    - Community connectivity
    - Resource enhancement
    - Multi-jurisdictional opportunities
    - Regional impacts
    - Interrelationships
- Ability to improve the community's quality of life
    - Community value
    - Livability

Each of the four categories that comprise the Cross-Cutting Benefits is described on the following pages.

The Project has significant positive...

Economic Impact

An area or community's economy can be affected for many months and even years after a disaster. At least one-fourth of all businesses that close because of a disaster never reopen. Small businesses are especially vulnerable because few of them have significant reserves to sustain a disruption in the economy. Businesses employ residents of the area and their closure can have a ripple effect on the area economy. Real estate and home construction, trade, agriculture and livestock - even the purchasing power of the dollar – may be impacted by an incident of national significance.

Therefore, it is important to implement projects that facilitate recovery by quickly improving economic conditions. Projects with significant economic impact can be defined as those that create jobs, reestablish critical infrastructure that allow the economy to function, and provide new economic opportunities for future generations. Those projects that encourage the highest and best economic use for the least amount of financial input will be given the most consideration. When assessing the positive economic impact of the project, the following questions will be kept in mind:

- Does the project help disaster victims get back to work?
- Does it help businesses reopen?
- Does it attract new business to the area or expand existing businesses.
- Does it provide new opportunities to improve previous economic conditions?

The Tool provides a framework for evaluating these questions and for determining the significance of a project's economic impact based on the following criteria:

Gets people back to work
- Job creation – re-establishes existing or provides new permanent jobs that can be filled by disaster victims or displaced workers.

Opens businesses
- Redevelopment – rebuilds or redevelops damaged properties using sustainable development measures.
- Business Space – provides new affordable opportunities for business owners to purchase property or building space and/or provides affordable lease opportunities for existing or new businesses.
- Revenue Generation – increases existing business incomes; contributes to additional spending.

New economic opportunities

- Diversify Economy / Encourage Emerging Markets – provide new opportunities to diversify the economy by establishing programs or capital projects (e.g. training facility; fiber optic infrastructure; distribution center) that would jump-start new industries.
- Training / Increased Wages – provides avenues for job training or apprenticeships that would lead to increased wages for skills in demand.
- Business Attraction – provides mechanisms to market area assets to potential industries.
- Increases Local Capacity – establishes economic development plans, new programs, or increases professional staff to facilitate economic growth.

The project has...

High Visibility and Builds Community Capacity

In the wake of a disastrous event, communities may temporarily receive extra attention and focus based on the impact of a disaster. A disaster may have visibility at a national level due to the disaster's significance or scale of impact and is certainly visible at the local level as the community and affected parties focus on the tasks, steps and actions to put their community back together.

As members of the community begin the process of recovery and return to a sense of normalcy, they also need a sense of community belonging and investment. A community's ability to see progress and change during the recovery process is an important part of the healing process. Ensuring a visible and measured process of long-term recovery can have a significant impact on personal courage and community spirit during a time of extreme stress and uncertainty.

The Tool provides a framework to evaluate "high visibility" projects as a result of a disaster. Project visibility is measured based on the following criteria:

Community Investment
- Investment – project receives financial or physical investment from a varied cross section of community members.

Awareness
- Awareness – includes projects that receive national interest through media attention, public agency support, etc.
- Recognition – projects with high visibility and distinct recognition within the community and/or projects that are landmarks or elements of significant interest or pride.

Catalyst Projects
- Foundation – projects that address key services within the community. Without these fundamental and essential public and private sector projects, elements, or services, the community would be limited in their ability to flourish (e.g. city hall; water distribution; waste hauling; facilities; post office; etc.).
- Significance – projects that play key roles in attracting other projects or developments.
- Financing – projects that attract or utilize multiple sources of financial support.

Multiple Impacts

- Market Sectors – projects that impact more than one market segment in a community, such as housing, retail, industry, etc.
- Geographic – projects that serve or support multiple geographic areas within a community or region.

Visionary

- Innovative – projects that use new or innovative technologies to produce creative solutions to complex or challenging situations. The determination to use innovative techniques should be measured against the provision of an efficient use of resources and maximizing public investment.
- Policy – projects that enhance or support significant changes in public policy or principles, such as the adoption of new or improved local codes or ordinances, mitigation of undesirable situations, removal of non-conforming structures, etc.

The project provides...

Linkages Throughout the Community and Connections to Other Projects & Funding Resources

Long-term recovery projects come in all forms, and each project is a result of a specific void created in the community as a result of a disaster. Individual recovery projects viewed in a broad context may have an impact beyond their original scope or purpose. During the recovery process it is essential that these "individual" projects be viewed as pieces of a larger puzzle – when linked together they create a stronger community framework. Developing a series of supportive projects, linked to other segments within the community can have a greater impact on recovery than individual or stand-alone projects.

Linkages not only refers to projects that have connections to other individual projects, but also to other aspects of the community – connections among people and services; neighborhoods and downtowns; urban and rural; local and regional.

The Tool provides a framework to evaluate "linkages" which are created from or supported by a project. The "linkage" of a project is measured based on the following criteria:

Community Connectivity
- Interconnectivity – includes projects that physically connect neighborhoods, key features, districts, services, or communities or provide less tangible connectivity within a community, e.g. a downtown revitalization project or other magnet project that would draw people from one area to another.

Resource Enhancement
- Community Resources – includes projects that support the existing resources of the community, including cultural, physical, natural, and environmental resources.

Multi-Jurisdictional Opportunities
- Interagency Cooperation – includes projects that are planned, developed, or implemented cooperatively among various local, state or federal agencies or organizations. Cooperation could include planning coordination, regulatory review, funding resources, or project implementation activities.

Regional Impacts
- Regional – includes projects of a regional nature that support areas beyond just the disaster-affected community.

Interrelationships

- ○ <u>Multiple Elements</u> – is related to other community projects, resources, or elements that complement one another and may be part of an overall strategy.

The Project...

Enhances the Quality of Life in the Community

A high quality of life is vital not only to the emotional well-being of a community, but also to its economic well-being. As part of their decision to relocate to an area, successful industries examine the quality of life in a community. People wishing to move their families to a new place examine its schools, hospitals, transportation systems, environment, recreational facilities, public safety, and amenities before making their final decision. If the social, health, economic, and environmental conditions are not acceptable, people will not relocate to the area.

Following a disaster, the community is vulnerable to economic instability as some residents relocate and businesses are forced to close or move to new areas. The community is also prone to significant quality of life degradations; e.g., traffic problems due to damages to traffic control systems, temporary housing developments that may impact surrounding land uses and create slum-like conditions for the tenants, and loss of important community icons such as a bandstand or community meeting hall. This makes the community less attractive to current residents, new businesses, and prospective residents. The housing shortage following a disaster makes it even harder for prospective residents to move to the community. Projects that improve the quality of life can have a direct impact on the decisions that businesses and people make regarding relocation.

In recognition of the important role that quality of life plays in a community, FEMA states that a community's "disaster mitigation and recovery resources should be invested to improve the quality of life in the areas of public health and safety, environmental stewardship, and social and economic security."

The framework for evaluating whether a project makes an important contribution to quality of life is based on the following criteria:

Enhances Community Value
- Promotes Existing Strengths within the Community – for example, these projects may build on existing tourism or attract additional growth to the area. Improvements in these previously successful areas may increase community resilience.

Increases the Livability of the Area
- Provides or Enhances Community Services – this includes schools, libraries, cultural centers, community gathering places, and recreational facilities.
- Provides or Enhances a Critical Facility – this includes hospitals, fire and police stations, and other emergency response facilities.

- Enhances Housing/Shelter Situations – this includes providing community shelters, enhancing mixed-income housing options, and improving assisted living facilities.
- Project Enhances a Culturally Significant Place – this can include historical properties, community gathering places or sites where events significant to the community took place.

IMPLEMENTATION OF PROJECT RECOVERY VALUE DESIGNATION

The Long-Term Community Recovery Planning Team will use the Recovery Value Tool as a guide to classify projects into one of the four recovery value categories (High, Moderate, Low, Community Interest) and then present the projects in a Long-Term Community Recovery Plan.

LTCR Report Format to Convey a Project's Recovery Value

Each project in the plan will be rated with the Recovery Value Tool. This recovery value will be highlighted within the project description. There should be a specific section in the project write-up that identifies the recovery value and provides a brief description of why the specific recovery value was chosen. In addition to the project write-up, additional methods for conveying the project recovery value could be employed as part of the plan:

1. **A table or matrix could be included at the beginning of the plan document that lists all projects by recovery value and incorporates a color scheme that differentiates those projects**. For example, all High Recovery Value projects could have a red band. The project listing in the Long Term Community Recovery Plan for Utica, IL is a good example of such a table. (The Utica example includes High, Moderate, and Community Interest Projects and also incorporates feedback from the community.)

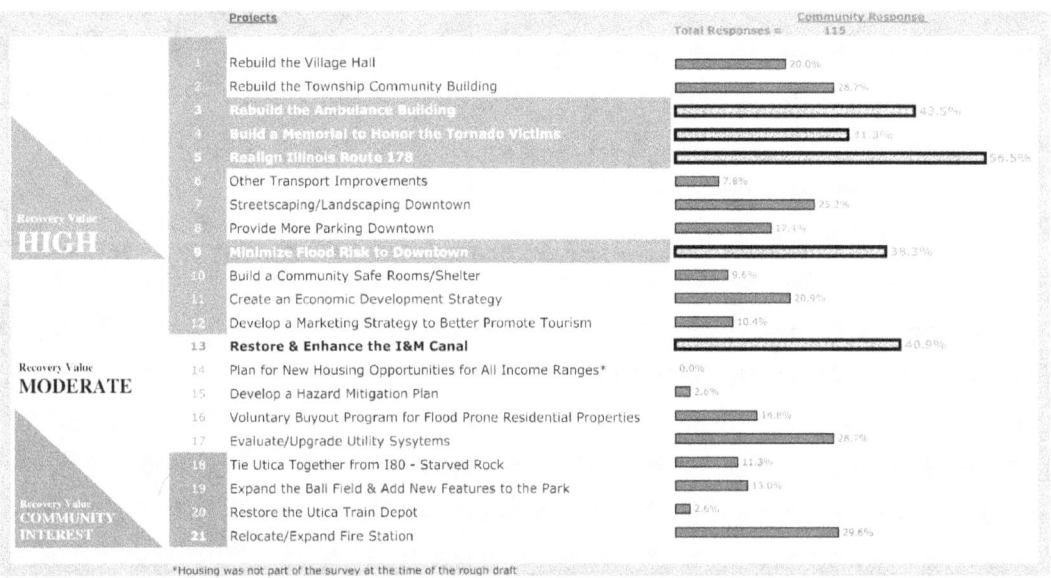

The table included in future LTCR plans should include High, Medium, and Low Recovery Value projects and Community Interest projects. Inclusion of the community's response to the projects, as was included in the Utica Plan document (shown on the right hand side of the table), will depend on the size of the community and the time available to incorporate that information. The page number for each project could also be included in the table.

2. **Each page containing a project description could be color-coded using the same colors as the table.** The color code could be in the form of a band along the outside edge of the page and should include the Recovery Value Designation; e.g., High Recovery Value, etc. The following colors are recommended.
   - ⏰ High Recovery Value – RED
   - ⏰ Moderate Recovery Value – YELLOW
   - ⏰ Low Recovery Value – GREEN
   - ⏰ Community Interest - BLUE

3. **A Communication Format to articulate a project's recovery value should also be used in the LTCR Plan document.** The following symbols are recommended:

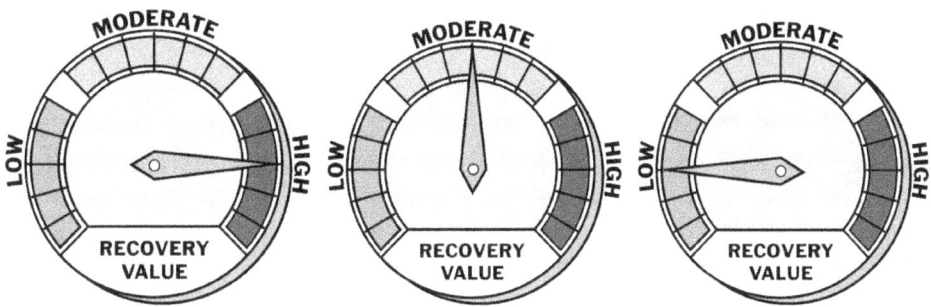

Community Interest

Summary of Recovery Value Concept

A summary of the Recovery Value concept should be included in the front page of each LTCR Plan to introduce the concept immediately. The summary could be taken from the definition section on page five of this guide. The following represents a summary of the Recovery Value concept that could be used in the front page of each LTCR Plan.

Recovery Value is the designation assigned to a project for its ability to help jump-start a community's recovery from a natural disaster or incident of national significance. Projects that contribute to recovery typically address a broad range of issues that contribute to a functioning and healthy economy, address infrastructure improvements, expand housing development, address environmental considerations, and revitalize downtowns.

Each project in this LTCR Plan has been assigned one of four Recovery Values:
  o High
  o Moderate
  o Low
  o Community Interest

Each project has undergone an assessment based on the following criteria and has been assigned a Recovery Value based on how well it meets the criteria:
  o Meets a Community Need
  o Is Sustainable
  o Is Feasible
  o Provides a Positive Overall Community Impact (in the following areas)
    ☺ Stimulates the Economy
    ☺ Provides Linkages
    ☺ Has High Visibility
    ☺ Contributes to the Community's Quality of Life

Those projects assigned a **high recovery value** are **catalyst projects that have multiple impacts** on the community and its recovery for recovery. Typically, a High Recovery Value project will:
  o Be directly related to damages
  o Have community support and community-wide benefits
  o Be achievable (within a 3-5 year recovery timeline) and sustainable
  o Have a champion
  o Incorporate identified best practices for reducing loss in the future
  o Create economic opportunities
  o Have a high visibility and build community capacity
  o Leverage and create linkages to other projects and resources
  o Enhance quality of life for the community

Additional information can be added to the above sample detailing the number of projects contained in the LTCR Plan, the number of High Recovery Value projects, etc.

<u>Funding Priorities</u>

The criteria for a high recovery value project are consistent with many of the funding criteria used for grant programs. It is important to convey the recovery value concept and the reasons for a project's designation to potential funding agencies and to the local community. A clear explanation of the recovery value concept and a brief summary of the key criteria addressed by a particular project will assist both the funding agencies and the local community as funds are sought to implement the projects.

Timing of Projects

Priority should be given to those projects that have the highest recovery value for a community. At the same time, it is important to have an immediate success with a project. In some instances, a high recovery value project may not be the first project undertaken, or at least completed, due to funding availability, complexity, etc. A community may want to complete a project that has high visibility and strong community support but a moderate or community interest recovery value in order to have an immediate success and sustain the community interest and support for Long-Term Recovery.

APPENDICES

APPENDIX I: Rating System (Spreadsheets)

This section contains the Recovery Value spreadsheet Tool for the following categories:

1. Meets a Post-Disaster Community Need
2. Project Feasibility
3. Sustainable Development
4. Economic Impact
5. High Visibility and Builds Community Capacity
6. Linkages throughout Community and Connections to Other Projects
7. Quality of Life

Long Term Recovery Assessment Tool

RECOVERY VALUE: Meets A Post-Disaster Community Need

<<< Insert name of Project and Jurisdiction here >>>

#	Criteria	Data Source	Data	Units	Score	Guidance Notes for Scoring	Notes
Direct Damages							
1	Project is directly related to physical damage(s) sustained in the disaster.					Score based on degree the project addresses physical damage sustained in the disaster. 1=**Low** match with criteria; 2=**Moderate** match w/ criteria; 3=**High** match with criteria.	
2	Project provides an opportunity to improve on pre-disaster conditions.					Score based on how project improves upon pre-disaster conditions. 1=**Low** match with criteria; 2=**Moderate** match w/ criteria; 3=**High** match with criteria.	
Fills A Gap							
3	Project addresses an issue or a need Identified in Other Plans (Comprehensive; Strategic; Neighborhood; Historic; Improvement District; etc.) or is validated or attains a new urgency as a result of the disaster.					Score based on how project addresses an issue or a need identified in existing plan(s) or studies for community. 1=**Low** match with criteria; 2=**Moderate** match w/ criteria; 3=**High** match with criteria.	Is the project called out in any existing plans or does the project address a specific community need or issue that is identified in plans, studies, reports?
4	Project is essential for the health and safety of the community.					Score based on how project provides direct impact on health and/or safety services within the community. 1=**Low** match with criteria; 2=**Moderate** match w/ criteria; 3=**High** match with criteria.	
Leverage							
5	Leverages several sources of funding.					Score based on project's potential to leverage several funding sources for its implementation, or provide leverage for funding of another project(s). 1=**Low** match with criteria; 2=**Moderate** match w/ criteria; 3=**High** match with criteria.	
Community Support and Impact							
6	Project is supported by the community.					Score based on degree the community support for project has been identified through referendum, surveys, or other documented methods of community support. 1=**Low** match with criteria; 2=**Moderate** match w/ criteria; 3=**High** match with criteria.	
7	Project impacts low-moderate income segment of community.					Score based on how project impacts low to moderate income households in community. 1=**Low** match with criteria; 2=**Moderate** match w/ criteria; 3=**High** match with criteria.	High match would be if at least 25% of households impacted by project have household income of less than 75% of median hh income in community.
8	Project affects key social or cultural component of community.					Score based on degree project affects distinct social or cultural attributes of the community. 1=**Low** match with criteria; 2=**Moderate** match w/ criteria; 3=**High** match with criteria.	
Meets a Need Average Recovery Value Score*		0					

* If any of the criteria above are not applicable, change the averaging formula to represent the number of criteria used. For example, total scores may need to be divided by 7 instead of 8.

Long Term Recovery Assessment Tool

RECOVERY VALUE: Project Feasibility

<< Insert name of Project and Jurisdiction here >>>

#	Criteria	Data Source	Data	Units	Score	Guidance Notes for Scoring	Notes
Builds Upon Available Resources							
1	Can access necessary resources.					Score based on probability of securing necessary funding **within project timeframe.** 1=**Low** match with criteria; 2=**Moderate** match w/ criteria; 3=**High** match with criteria.	With necessary resources, project cannot be completed; if scaling back is required for budgetary reasons (and scaled-back project meets project requirements), then project will have access to all necessary funding and other resources (e.g., in-kind, staff, office space, supplies, volunteers, etc).
Conforms to Regulatory, Logistical, and Planning Constraints							
2	Compatible with Government Initiatives and local plans.					Score based on degree project is compatible with government initiatives and/or local plans. 1=**Low** match with criteria; 2=**Moderate** match w/ criteria; 3=**High** match with criteria.	Not in conflict with other planning efforts/projects, whether recovery related or part of pre-existing community development initiatives; supports and enhances other planning activities.
3	Project addresses an issue or a need. Identified in Other Plans (Comprehensive; Strategic; Neighborhood; Historic; Improvement District; etc.) or is validated or attains a new urgency as a result of the disaster.					Score based on project's consistency with existing ordinances and/or regulations. 1=**Low** match with criteria; 2=**Moderate** match w/ criteria; 3=**High** match with criteria.	Not in conflict with existing statues or regulations.
Is Achievable							
4	Definable Outcomes.					Score based on degree project has clearly defined outcomes. 1=**Low** match with criteria; 2=**Moderate** match w/ criteria; 3=**High** match with criteria.	If outcomes are not clear, project could become a resource drain that stretches indefinitely into the future. It could indicate high potential for conflict among project partners.
5	Workable Timeframe.					Score based on how project timeframe fits both immediate community need and needs of other possibly related projects. 1=**Low** match with criteria; 2=**Moderate** match w/ criteria; 3=**High** match with criteria.	A "reasonable and practical timeframe" is one that is responsive to community need, that is compatible with other planning efforts (especially if those efforts rely on this project's completion), and that can be achieved within the limits of available resources.
6	Other Characteristics Affecting Project Feasibility (e.g., design or plan flexibility, ease of implementation, political support, etc).					As applicable, score based on how aspects or characteristics of the project have a positive affect on the project's feasibility. 1=**Low** match with criteria; 2=**Moderate** match w/ criteria; 3=**High** match with criteria.	This is a place in which to acknowledge the importance of other characteristics affecting project feasibility. This might include design or plan flexibility, ease of implementation, offering a sufficient range of options that will increase the likelihood of project success, etc. This criterion is intentionally left open to interpretation to accommodate unique project characteristics.
Has a Champion							
7	Identified Committed Champion.					Score based on whether committed project champion(s) has been identified (see definition in notes). 1=**Low** match with criteria; 2=**Moderate** match w/ criteria; 3=**High** match with criteria.	A project "champion" is an individual (or group) with sufficient enthusiasm, political influence, and access to resources to get the project done. Without this person steering the project, it has very low likelihood of being completed.
Feasibility Average Recovery Value Score*				0			

* If any of the criteria above are not applicable, change the averaging formula to represent the number of criteria used. For example, total scores may need to be divided by 6 instead of 7.

Long Term Recovery Assessment Tool

RECOVERY VALUE: Sustainable Development

<<< Insert name of Project and Jurisdiction here >>>

#	Criteria	Data Source	Data	Units	Score	Guidance Notes for Scoring	Notes
Financially Sustainable							
1	Project demonstrates that it can pay for itself over the long-term.					Score based on degree construction and/or operation estimates of the project demonstrate that it would pay for itself over time or that it can be financed by the local government without additional aid over the long term (includes possible outside grant/loan funds). 1=**Low** match with criteria; 2=**Moderate** match w/ criteria; 3=**High** match with criteria.	
Averts Future Loss							
2	Project identified in existing Mitigation or Safety Plans.	Local or State Jurisdiction				Score based on degree that project is identified in existing plan(s) for community or if project employs techniques set forth in existing plans. 1=Low match with criteria; 2=Moderate match w/ criteria; 3=High match with criteria.	A specific project may be identified, or a mitigation technique identified, in an existing plan that may be used in the project. For example, a housing project that employs mitigation construction techniques.
3	Project addresses an issue or a need Identified in Other Plans (Comprehensive; Strategic; Neighborhood; Historic; Improvement District; etc.) or is validated or attains a new urgency as a result of the disaster.	Federal, State, or Local Mitigation or Public Safety Handbooks				Score based on degree project employs proven/previously tested mitigation or safety measure OR if an assigned recovery professional (such as an engineer; architect; planner; geologist; landscape architect; or urban designer) determine that the project would reduce or alleviate future disasters or improve public security in the future. 1=**Low** match with criteria; 2=**Moderate** match w/ criteria; 3=**High** match with criteria.	Examples of proven methods include typical hazard mitigation projects such as: relocating a structure, restricting new construction in particularly vulnerable areas, elevating structures to remove the threat of flooding, building smarter, stronger buildings and utilities that are more hazard-resistant, or security enhancement.
Built and Natural Resource Efficiency							
4	Project promotes efficient use of land.	Low Impact Development Center; Federal Sustainable Development program criteria; Smart Growth Online; USDA Rural Development				Score based on degree project advances sustainable development; low impact development; or smart growth principles. Smart growth principles may include encouraging vertical over horizontal development; brownfield, greyfield, or infill development; mixed use and /or mixed income neighborhoods; limiting urban sprawl; or other like principles. 1=**Low** match with criteria; 2=**Moderate** match w/ criteria; 3=**High** match with criteria.	
5	Project is geographically located to encourage safe, convenient, and efficient connectivity with other nodes of development within the community.					Score based on how project is situated within the geographic context of the community to ensure a safe, convenient and efficient system of connections within the community. 1=**Low** match with criteria; 2=**Moderate** match w/ criteria; 3=**High** match with criteria.	
6	Project protects or does not harm key ecosystems; wildlife and natural areas; and / or improves water and air quality.	State Dept of Natural Resources; USDA Natural Resources Conservation Service				Score based on degree project advances the preservation of natural areas; restores or protects key ecosystems, or improves water or air quality. 1=**Low** match with criteria; 2=**Moderate** match w/ criteria; 3=**High** match with criteria.	
7	Project reduces water and energy use; and / or employs innovative wastewater technologies.	State Dept of Natural Resources; Environmental Protection Agency				Score based on degree project addresses reduction of energy or water use, improves stormwater flow, or addresses wastewater quality from previous conditions. 1=**Low** match with criteria; 2=**Moderate** match w/ criteria; 3=**High** match with criteria.	
8	Project improves availability of mass transit or advances multiple transportation solutions for those who need it.	Federal, state or local transportation agencies				Score based on how project addresses opportunities for mass transit or advances multiple transportation solutions that would reduce the dependency on cars or single transportation modes. 1=**Low** match with criteria; 2=**Moderate** match w/ criteria; 3=**High** match with criteria.	

Sustainable Development Average Recovery Value Score*				0		

* If any of the criteria above are not applicable, change the averaging formula to represent the number of criteria used. For example, total scores may need to be divided by 7 instead of 8.

Long Term Recovery Assessment Tool

RECOVERY VALUE: Economic Impact

<<< Insert name of Project and Jurisdiction here >>>

#	Criteria	Data Source	Data	Units	Score	Guidance Notes for Scoring	Notes
	Gets people back to work						
1	Project creates job opportunities.	State Input-Output (I/O) Tables or Estimate of Job creation				Score based on degree project creates more direct jobs on a specific site than were lost as a result of the disaster and has a multiplier effect on other employment. 1=**Low** match with criteria; 2=**Moderate** match w/ criteria; 3=**High** match with criteria.	Multipliers are determined regionally. Each state has specific I/O tables that identify employment multipliers per industry. High impact would be a project that has an employment multiplier of > 1.5 per direct job. If no state multipliers are available, estimate job creation impact of project.
	Opens businesses						
2	Project rebuilds or redevelops damaged properties.					Score based on degree project rebuilds or redevelops damaged properties using sustainable development measures. 1=**Low** match with criteria; 2=**Moderate** match w/ criteria; 3=**High** match with criteria.	
3	Project addresses an issue or a need Identified in Other Plans (Comprehensive; Strategic; Neighborhood; Historic; Improvement District; etc.) or is validated or attains a new urgency as a result of the disaster.					Score based on degree project provides new opportunities for business owners to purchase property or building space and/or provides affordable leasing or rent opportunities. 1=**Low** match with criteria; 2=**Moderate** match w/ criteria; 3=**High** match with criteria.	"Affordable" should be based upon the average $/SF cost of business space prior to disaster and the average lease/rent rate prior to disaster.
4	Project contributes to increased income / revenues for new and existing businesses.	Estimates based on previous municipal finance conditions				Score based on estimate that the project would increase tax revenues, business incomes, or the circulation of money within the economy more than prior to the disaster event. 1=**Low** match with criteria; 2=**Moderate** match w/ criteria; 3=**High** match with criteria.	
	New economic opportunities						
5	Project would further diversify the economy by encouraging emerging markets into the region.					Score based on degree that the project would encourage new employment opportunities by establishing new capital projects (e.g. training facility; fiber optic infrastructure; distribution center) that would jump-start new industries in a region where an emerging market could be fostered. 1=**Low** match with criteria; 2=**Moderate** match w/ criteria; 3=**High** match with criteria.	
6	Project would improve the skillset of the labor force / increase wages.					Score based on whether project provides new training programs and / or facilities that would allow labor force to learn new skills that are in demand. 1=**Low** match with criteria; 2=**Moderate** match w/ criteria; 3=**High** match with criteria.	
7	Project would provide marketing mechanisms for business attraction.					Score based on degree project provides a marketing program or creates regional entities that would market area assets to new businesses, industry, or market segments. 1=**Low** match with criteria; 2=**Moderate** match w/ criteria; 3=**High** match with criteria.	
8	Project would increase local capacity for economic development.					Score based on degree project establishes an economic development plan, new programs (e.g. GIS software), or increases professional staff to facilitate economic growth. 1=**Low** match with criteria; 2=**Moderate** match w/ criteria; 3=**High** match with criteria.	

Average Economic Average Recovery Value Score*	0

* If any of the criteria above are not applicable, change the averaging formula to represent the number of criteria used. For example, total scores may need to be divided by 7 instead of 8.

Long Term Recovery Assessment Tool

RECOVERY VALUE: High Visibility and Builds Community Capacity

<<< Insert name of Project and Jurisdiction here >>>

#	Criteria	Data Source	Data	Units	Score	Guidance Notes for Scoring	Notes
Community Investment							
1	Project fosters community investment from local citizens; businesses; and local governing bodies.					Score based on degree project has received or will continue to receive community investment - financial, physical, and in-kind from various segments of the community. 1=**Low** match with criteria; 2=**Moderate** match w/ criteria; 3=**High** match with criteria.	
Awareness							
2	Project has the ability to create national interest through media attention, public agency support, regional impact, recognition, etc.					Score based on degree project has received national media interest or public agency support over a sustained period of time (6 months or more) or if the project is of such magnitude to undoubtedly attract sustained national interest. 1=**Low** match with criteria; 2=**Moderate** match w/ criteria; 3=**High** match with criteria.	
3	Project addresses an issue or a need Identified in Other Plans (Comprehensive; Strategic; Neighborhood; Historic; Improvement District; etc.) or is validated or attains a new urgency as a result of the disaster.					Score based on degree project has distinct and immediate recognition within and among the community. 1=**Low** match with criteria; 2=**Moderate** match w/ criteria; 3=**High** match with criteria.	This is identified in community promotional materials, publications or documents.
Catalyst Projects							
4	Project address key services within the community and without this project the community would be limited in their ability to flourish (e.g. city hall; water distribution; waste hauling; facilities; post office; etc.).					Score based on degree project has a direct and positive impact on the infrastructure or key services in the community. 1=**Low** match with criteria; 2=**Moderate** match w/ criteria; 3=**High** match with criteria.	Without these fundamental and essential public and private sector projects, elements or services the community would be limited in their ability to flourish.
5	Project is a catalyst to attract significant interest, projects, developments, resources or opportunities to the community (if not for this project, others would not follow).					Score on project's potential to attract significant resources or development opportunities to the community. 1=**Low** match with criteria; 2=**Moderate** match w/ criteria; 3=**High** match with criteria.	
6	Has potential to attract multiple sources of financial support - both public and private - at the local, regional, or national levels.					Score based on degree to which project involves public and private investment. 1=**Low** match with criteria; 2=**Moderate** match w/ criteria; 3=**High** match with criteria.	
Multiple Impacts							
7	Impacts more than one market segment within the community (e.g. housing, retail, industry, etc).					Score based on market segments affected as a result of the project. 1=**Low** match with criteria; 2=**Moderate** match w/ criteria; 3=**High** match with criteria.	A project receiving a High Score should affect at least two different market segments.
8	Serves or supports multiple geographic areas within a community or region.					Score based on degree project serves or supports several geographic areas within the community or region. 1=**Low** match with criteria; 2=**Moderate** match w/ criteria; 3=**High** match with criteria.	
Visionary							
9	Project is visionary and encourages the community to look beyond established patterns, tendencies and framework in search of forward thinking solutions and/or is creative and uses new techniques or methodologies to address issues or produce solutions.					Score based on degree project incorporates new design technologies or construction methodologies. 1=**Low** match with criteria; 2=**Moderate** match w/ criteria; 3=**High** match with criteria.	For example - sustainable projects; grand or majestic projects - sustainable technologies; recycled principles; green building; green roof; etc.
10	Project enhances or supports changes in public policy.					Score based on degree project enhances or supports changes in public policy or principles, such as the adoption of new or improved local codes or ordinances, mitigation of undesirable situations, removal of non-conforming structures, etc. 1=**Low** match with criteria; 2=**Moderate** match w/ criteria; 3=**High** match with criteria.	
High Visibility Average Recovery Value Score*				0			

* If any of the criteria above are not applicable, change the averaging formula to represent the number of criteria used. For example, total scores may need to be divided by 9 instead of 10.

Long Term Recovery Assessment Tool

RECOVERY VALUE: Linkages Throughout Community & Connection to Other Projects

<<Insert name of Project and Jurisdiction here   >>>

#	Criteria	Data Source	Data	Units	Score	Guidance Notes for Scoring	Notes
Community Connectivity							
1	Project is interconnected among and within the existing community development framework and physically connects neighborhoods, key features, districts, etc.					Score based on degree project physically connects neighborhoods, key features, districts, services, or communities or provides other less tangible connectivity within the community; e.g. downtown revitalization project or other magnet-type project that would draw people from one area to another. 1=Low match with criteria; 2=Moderate match w/ criteria; 3=High match with criteria.	
Resource Enhancement							
2	Project supports the existing resources of the community.					Score based on degree project supports existing resources of the community, including cultural, physical, natural, and environmental resources. 1=Low match with criteria; 2=Moderate match w/ criteria; 3=High match with criteria.	
	Project addresses an issue or a need Identified in Other Plans (Comprehensive; Strategic; Neighborhood; Historic; Improvement District; etc.) or is validated or attains a new urgency as a result of the disaster.						
3	Projects that are planned, developed, or implemented cooperatively.					Score based on whether the project planning, development, or implementation involves two or more local, state, or federal agencies or organizations. 1=Low match with criteria; 2=Moderate match w/ criteria; 3=High match with criteria.	Cooperation can include planning coordination, regulatory review, funding resources, or project implementation activities. Project should involve at least two agencies for a **High Score.**
Regional Impacts							
4	Project has an impact on the region or other regional projects.					Score based on the degree project is regional in scope or supports other regional projects. 1=Low match with criteria; 2=Moderate match w/ criteria; 3=High match with criteria.	
Interrelationships							
5	Related to other community projects, resources, or elements.					Score based on degree project is related to other community projects, resources, or elements that complement one another and are part of an overall recovery strategy. 1=Low match with criteria; 2=Moderate match w/ criteria; 3=High match with criteria.	
Linkages Average Recovery Value Score*	0						

* If any of the criteria above are not applicable, change the averaging formula to represent the number of criteria used. For example, total scores may need to be divided by 4 instead of 5.

Long Term Recovery Assessment Tool

RECOVERY VALUE: Quality of Life

<<< Insert name of Project and Jurisdiction here >>>

#	Criteria	Data Source	Data	Units	Score	Guidance Notes for Scoring	Notes
Enhances Community Value							
1	Project will promote an existing strength in the community and build resilience; e.g. project helps improve a facility or attraction that has improved the quality of life (monetarily or emotionally) for the community in the past and will continue to provide enhanced living for the community.					Score based on how project builds on an existing strength that the community has already been successfully promoting.1=**Low** match with criteria; 2=**Moderate** match w/ criteria; 3=**High** match with criteria.	
Livability							
2	Project provides or enhances community services (e.g. schools, libraries, cultural gathering places, and recreational facilities).	Needs assessment				Score based on degree project provides or enhances a badly needed (identified, unmeet need, or other) service that benefits a cross-section of the population (cross-section would include low income, minority, elderly, etc.). 1=**Low** match with criteria; 2=**Moderate** match w/ criteria; 3=**High** match with criteria.	
3	Project addresses an issue or a need Identified in Other Plans (Comprehensive; Strategic; Neighborhood; Historic; Improvement District; etc.) or is validated or attains a new urgency as a result of the disaster.					Score based on how project provides or enhances a critical facility that impacts the lives of the community; 1=**Low** match with criteria; 2=**Moderate** match w/ criteria; 3=**High** match with criteria.	
4	Project enhances housing/shelter situations (e.g. assisted living, mixed-income housing, disaster shelter).	Needs assessment				Score based on degree project fills an identified need. 1=**Low** match with criteria; 2=**Moderate** match w/ criteria; 3=**High** match with criteria.	
5	Project enhances a culturally significant place in the community.	Public meetings; City, County, or State lists of "cultural monuments"				Score based on degree project enhances a documented culturally significant place in the community (or one identified in public meetings). 1=**Low** match with criteria; 2=**Moderate** match w/ criteria; 3=**High** match with criteria.	
Quality of Life Average Recovery Value Score*				0			

* If any of the criteria above are not applicable, change the averaging formula to represent the number of criteria used. For example, total scores may need to be divided by 4 instead of 5.

Long Term Recovery Assessment Tool

Recovery Value: Summary Results

<< Insert name of Project and Jurisdiction here >>>

Category	Average Recovery Value Score
Meets a Post-Disaster Need	0
Project Feasibility	0
Sustainable Development	0
Economic Impact	0
High Visibility	ensive; Strategic; Neighborhood; Historic; Improvement District;
Linkages & Connection to Other Projects	0
Quality of Life	0
Project Recovery Value Score	**#VALUE!**
	#VALUE!

High Recovery Value
A High Recovery Value score results when the following occurs:
A project scores an average of 2.5 or higher

Moderate Recovery Value
A Moderate Recovery Value score results when the following occurs:
A project scores an average of 1.5 to 2.4

Low Recovery Value
A Low Recovery Value score results when the following occurs:
A project scores an average of 1.4 or less

Community Interest
A Community Interest score results when a project obtains a low recovery value designation but there is strong community support for the project. These projects generally cannot be implemented in a timeframe to affect recovery or may not clearly promote key disaster recovery goals.

APPENDICES

APPENDIX II: Application of Recovery Value Tool on Recent LTCR Projects

This section contains a description of recent LTCR projects for the 12 subject areas noted below. The Recovery Value Tool was applied to each of the projects described in the following pages. The worksheets are included on the enclosed compact disc. The worksheets include notes and comments documenting the reasons for the score.

- Housing
- Economic Development
- Government Facilities
- Infrastructure
- Health
- Education
- Agriculture
- Transportation
- Utilities
- Urban Planning
- Parks and Recreation
- Tourism

Housing

Repair and Build Housing for Renters - Santa Rosa County, Florida
Recovery Value: High

Hurricane Ivan struck the Gulf Coast of Florida and Alabama in September of 2004 and affected more than 23,000 households in Santa Rosa County. Approximately 827 affordable rental units were either damaged or destroyed. The LTCR team proposed a *Repair and Build Housing for Renters* project to build 827 affordable rental housing units 12-24 months post disaster. This project identified possible housing strategies to repair rental housing and assured that rental units would be available to meet demand after FEMA assistance expired. The estimated cost for the project was $9.5 million, with $7.5 million for a rental rehabilitation loan program and $2 million to buy down debt.

The plan proposed the following action steps:

- *Rehabilitation assistance to property owners*: Provide financial assistance to owners of affordable rental housing to assist in repair. Financial assistance may include gap financing, very low interest loans and deferred loans. The incorporated areas of the county should establish a revolving loan fund for rehabilitation of affordable rental housing units, which would be offered to property owners not eligible for SBA loans or who have a financing gap. Disbursement agreements from this fund would require the receiver to rent at pre-disaster rates. The maximum loan amount per unit would be $10,000.
- *Buy down debt*: Santa Rosa County should consider establishing a deferred loan program to provide incentives for affordable property owners to repair and rebuild. The loans will be exclusively used to buy down existing debt on the development to the point where it is feasible to set rental rates for affordable housing. Many state and federal programs are available to provide developers and non-profits with rebuilding grants or loans and are listed in the original Santa Rosa Long-Term Recovery Plan.
- *Rental subsidies*: Although not specifically a repair rental housing strategy, the need for additional rental subsidies should be addressed and the county should pursue additional allocations based on this need. The rental subsidies available for Santa Rosa County are listed in the original Santa Rosa Long-Term Recovery Project proposal.

Economic Development

**Improve Telecommunications and Internet Access – A Regional
Project for Charlotte, DeSoto and Hardee Counties in Florida.
Recovery Value: High**

The hurricanes of 2004 affected a large section of south central Florida.
Although the disaster presented many challenges, it also provided
opportunities for Charlotte, DeSoto and Hardee Counties to combine their
efforts on projects with a regional impact that could not be undertaken by a
single entity. This particular project is one of many included in the LTR Plan
that has the ability to build unprecedented cooperation and collectively
leverage the region's influence for long-term recovery.

This project proposes an evaluation of the existing telecommunications
system in coordination with the state, counties, regional economic
development entities, and private partners. A plan would result from this to
include identification of desired systems (broadband, wireless technologies,
etc.), identification of desired infrastructure options (cell towers, fiber optic
cable, etc.) and establishment of a strategy for phasing in the
telecommunication upgrades. This project is identified in the state's strategic
plan for economic development of rural areas and is consistent with the
mission of Florida's High-Tech Corridor Council.

The tri-county area is well positioned to incorporate a fiber-optic backbone
for a network to connect to Florida's High-Tech Corridor along US 17. By
expanding this designated corridor to Charlotte County, an infrastructure
project will link Charlotte, DeSoto, and Hardee counties to the
Tampa/Sarasota/Orlando/Space Coast High Technology Corridor. This crucial
link will advance educational opportunities and training programs, and
increase higher-wage job opportunities and the quality of life for residents.

The estimated planning cost is $200,000.

Government Facilities

Rebuild City Hall
Pierce City, Missouri
Recovery Value: High

In May of 2003, an F3 tornado touched down in Pierce City and caused catastrophic damage throughout the community – including the destruction of 42 out of 45 downtown businesses. City Hall was located downtown and suffered such extreme damage that it was deemed unsafe for occupancy and demolished. City Hall had occupied a 3,000 square foot building that housed most of the city's administrative functions, including the mayor, city clerk, municipal court and the police office. After the tornado, all of these functions were moved off-site to a trailer.

The project proposes three options for rebuilding City Hall. The first option would leave City Hall as is – operating out of a trailer. The second option proposes rebuilding City Hall in its previous location. The new building would need to be elevated at an additional cost of $40,000, because it would reside in a flood plain. The third option proposes relocating City Hall to a new 29,000 square feet of property that the city would need to acquire on Commercial Street. The original train station located adjacent to this site, but demolished more than 20 years ago, would inspire the design of the 3,200 square foot building. If located here, City Hall would recapture a historically significant site and help define a downtown activity center comprised of the existing Gulf War Memorial, a fountain, and the bandstand across the street. As this property is also in a floodplain, the building would need to be elevated at a cost of $45,000.

The first option requires $18,553 in additional funding, which is covered by insurance. The estimated cost for the second option is $410,537, which is covered by insurance and FEMA Disaster Assistance. The cost of the third option is $455,530, and $44,993 of that cost is not covered by existing funding resources.

Infrastructure

DeSoto Co., FL: Improve Water, Wastewater and Stormwater Systems

Recovery Value: High

Hurricane Ivan damaged portions of the water and wastewater systems in DeSoto County and the City of Arcadia. The capacity and reliability of these systems affect economic growth and viability in the City of Arcadia and in DeSoto County. This project proposes improvements to existing wastewater and stormwater infrastructure to position the county for future growth and economic development. The purpose of this project is to provide reliable water and sewer systems within the City of Arcadia and DeSoto County, and reduce flood loss. The project has two parts, each of which may be implemented as resources allow:

- ⊕ Preparation of a Utility Master Plan and Feasibility Study for both DeSoto County and the City of Arcadia - Evaluate existing water, wastewater and stormwater systems.
- ⊕ Improve the water distribution system for the City of Arcadia.

Elements of both components are included in the full DeSoto County Long-Term Recovery Plan.

The estimated cost for both components of the Improve Water, Wastewater, and Stormwater Systems Project is $29.6 million. The major costs include improvements to Arcadia's water distribution system ($10 million), upgrades to Arcadia's wastewater treatment facility ($8 million), upgrades to Arcadia's water treatment plant ($5 million), and upgrades to Arcadia's water collection system ($5 million).

Health

Rebuild Health Department & Clinic
Stockton, Missouri
Recovery Value: High

A tornado left the city of Stockton, Missouri with a third of its downtown businesses in ruins and over 200 homes destroyed. The Clinic and Health Department offices were also completely destroyed. This was especially devastating given that the average per capita income of community residents was $17,039, a number 58% below the national average. The Cedar County Health Department and the Cedar County Hospital Medical Center were both public services that operated from a single location under the administration of Cedar County Hospital in El Dorado Springs. Prior to the tornado, the lack of health services in Stockton was expressed as a concern by residents through an April 1993 opinion survey of community needs conducted by the Missouri Department of Economic Development. The issue was raised again post-disaster.

The Health Department was only open 2 days per week, while the Clinic provided full medical services, excluding overnight stays and most operations. The facility was located downtown in several converted retail units totaling 14,000 square feet. The hospital owned the property and buildings, which were totally destroyed. The Clinic and Health Department offices are currently located in temporary modular offices with about 4,000 square feet of space on the site of a hospital owned nursing home. The facility's minimum space need is 10,000 square feet, and they had an existing plan to build a 20,000 square foot facility with leased spaces that could be rented until needed by the hospital. They also indicated a desire to consider construction on a vacant portion of the nursing home site.

The LTR team proposed three options for the Clinic and Health Department. The facility could remain in a modular housing facility on the nursing home grounds. The facility could also rebuild on the existing site. However, this would not provide room for future growth and exacerbated downtown parking problems. Option 3 involved rebuilding the facility at a new location and constructing a 20,000 square foot building, thus providing room for the Clinic to accommodate the expected increase in demand for its services over the next few years.

The estimated cost of remaining in the modular home is $2,000 per month, all of which is covered by insurance. Reconstruction on the original site would cost approximately $1.2 million, which would be covered by a combination of insurance and FEMA disaster assistance. The third option to build the new site would cost approximately $3.2 million.

Educational Opportunities

School Facilities
Charlotte County, Florida
Recovery Value: Moderate

Several school-owned facilities in Charlotte County were damaged or completely destroyed during Hurricane Ivan. Community facilities are an essential component of a high quality life and sense of community. The Charlotte High School is especially important to the community not just because many community members attended the school, but also because of its statewide significance as the first integrated high school in Florida. It is also on the National Register of Historic Places and is a significant landmark in the area. While the hurricane caused millions of dollars of damage to the high school, it also provided an opportunity to improve and upgrade the facilities.

The goal of this project is to rebuild adequate school facilities while retaining a sense of community history, and to provide resources to surrounding neighborhoods to assist in revitalization. It is also part of a larger Community Facility project, which includes rebuilding or restoring parts of the high school that were damaged or destroyed in the hurricane, including:

- The restoration of the high school's façade and construction of a new facility within the historical façade.
- Construction of a new graduation facility – high school graduates currently use facilities outside of the county to accommodate the over 6,000 graduation ceremony attendees, but these facilities were destroyed in the hurricane.
- Replacement of Baker Center – this was the site of many community development programs and was completely destroyed in the hurricane. Replacement of this center is also important to the revitalization of the East Punta Gorda area.

The restoration of the façade is already underway with $900,000 of existing funding and needs $4.6 million of addition funding to replace the facility inside. This includes the cost of building an auditorium for graduation and other uses. Replacement of the Baker center will cost $2.1 million.

Agriculture
**Build Research Center and Demonstration Farm on
Reclaimed Mining Land
Hardee County, Florida
Recovery Value: Community Interest**

Before the hurricanes, Hardee County faced slow economic growth, an unemployment rate of 8.6% and one of the lowest income levels in the state. Post-disaster, the county has a chance to increase the standard of living, create jobs, and generate economic growth. Thus, long-term economic recovery is integrated into many of the projects proposed, including the building of a research center and demonstration farm on reclaimed mining land.

Continuation of agriculture pursuits is of great community interest in Hardee County. Over the next 30 years, nearly 300,000 acres of land will be reclaimed from phosphate mining activities. The full extent of agricultural products that can be produced on reclaimed mining lands is unknown, thus, creation of a research center to study this phenomenon and determine how to maximize agricultural production on this type of land would serve many beneficial purposes and create an economic opportunity for the community. The goal of this project is to conduct large-scale scale studies on traditional agriculture crops, alternative crops, and agriculture technologies to determine the best use for reclaimed mine land. The project would accomplish this by developing an agricultural research and development center and a demonstration farm on reclaimed mining land to study the use of these lands, particularly for high value-added enterprises such as aquaculture and horticulture. Representatives from the phosphate industry and the University of Florida met to discuss this project and both are interested in participating.

The estimated cost of this project is approximately $1.5 million, including equipment, overhead and labor.

Transportation

Realign Illinois Route 178 – Utica, Illinois
Recovery Value: High

A tornado nearly leveled the downtown of Utica, Illinois on April 20th, 2004. The catastrophic damage to many downtown buildings created an opportunity to realign a major highway that actually passed through the downtown, clogging city streets, creating noise and occasional danger for pedestrians. An estimated 600 trucks passed through downtown Utica on a typical business day. Truck navigation on the narrow downtown streets, with sharp angled turns, generated conflicts for passenger vehicles and pedestrians. Separating truck and car traffic downtown, in conjunction with complementary transportation/streetscaping improvements, would enhance the business setting and improve the pedestrian environment, while maximizing the efficiency of traffic flow through the community.

This project provides a transportation right-of-way that is sensitive to the community's rebuilding plans, promotes a higher level of service and traffic safety, and minimizes the negative impacts of truck traffic through the community. At a minimum, the right-of-way corridor along the proposed alignment must be preserved in the short-term through an advance right-of-way acquisition project. At the request of the Village, the Illinois Department of Transportation (IDOT) agreed to conduct a Feasibility Study on the realignment of Illinois Route 178 (IL-178). Realignment of IL-178 would straighten the alignment, routing traffic 1 to 2 blocks west of downtown Utica. The Illinois Department of Transportation (IDOT) had already planned to realign Route 178, but the plans are on hold until IDOT completes a detailed study of the project area and obtains design approval and funding. The final project scope and limits will be determined through a detailed preliminary engineering study. This project has two phases:

- *Right-of-way acquisition*: Finalize the roadway corridor studies and complete sufficient engineering work to undertake an advance right-of-way acquisition project. Top priority should be given to tornado-damaged properties, so that rebuilding decisions can be expedited. If necessary, acquisition of undamaged properties can be deferred.
- *Construction*: The proposed IL-178 realignment would be most cost-effectively constructed as a single project from the CSX railroad crossing to the tie-in with the existing highway just south of the I&M Canal, including a new bridge over the canal.

The cost for the right-of-way acquisition is $1.4 million. Construction costs are estimated at $3.1 million, to include a 2-lane state highway, an 80' bridge, railroad crossing, utilities, traffic control, landscaping, and design and engineering.

Utilities

Improve or Replace Main Street Wastewater Treatment Plant and Site Redevelopment – Escambia County, FL
Recovery Value: High

Hurricane Ivan struck Escambia County and the City of Pensacola in 2004 and this project is an example of an opportunity created by the disaster. The Main Street Waste Water Treatment Plant (WWTP) was built on Pensacola's waterfront. Even before the storm, the plant had flooding and odor problems, and contributed to air pollution and poor water quality downtown. Furthermore, it utilized outdated technology and was in need of an upgrade. As a result of its location in a flood plain and storm-related system failures, millions of gallons of untreated sewage flowed into Downtown streets and Pensacola Bay during and after Hurricane Ivan.

This project calls for either repairing or replacing (and hardening) the WWTP that was significantly damaged in the hurricane. This aging plant occupies 18.5 acres in the center of the downtown waterfront. Upgrading or moving the plant would eliminate the direct discharge of treated effluent into Pensacola Bay and was identified as a top priority of Pensacola citizens. This plan proposes three options for redevelopment/improvement of the WWTP:

- *Repair and upgrade existing WWTP*: Upgrade the facility to meet present environmental codes and standards. However, a full upgrade to current codes may not be possible due to the lack of room on the site for a reject storage pond. Estimated cost: $68.5 million.
- *Replace and improve WWTP*: This option would eliminate millions of gallons per day of treated effluent from release into Pensacola Bay by incorporating the use of wetlands and state of the art technology to increase effluent quality and minimize flow to rivers and estuaries. Furthermore, it identifies local industrial re-users of treated effluent and would eliminate future storm-induced damage. Estimated cost: $175 million.
- *Site redevelopment*: Existing Escambia County plans seek to reunite Downtown Pensacola with its waterfront through a number of community-led redevelopment initiatives, many of which were underway before the hurricane struck. This facility sits on land that has an extremely high development potential and that has the capacity to benefit the community more than its current use. A new treatment facility located elsewhere in Escambia County will make the 18.5-acre Main Street site available for redevelopment.

The estimated cost to repair and upgrade the plant is $68.5 million, while the estimated cost to replace and improve the plant is $175 million. $84 million was raised for the project prior to this proposal in the Long-Term Recovery Plan. Funds were a mix of State Tribal Assistance Grants and Loans, State and Regional Funds, and ECUA local funds.

Urban Planning
Wauchula, Hardee Co., FL: Downtown Revitalization Study
Recovery Value: High

Wauchula was the economic center of Hardee County before nearly one-third of its businesses suffered severe hurricane damage, and many closed indefinitely. The estimated total damage to the city was $50 million, a loss that was estimated to result in a city revenue decrease of 15%. Similar conditions existed in Hardee County's other towns, Zolfo Springs and Bowling Green. This project will improve the business climate; enrich the lives of counties' residents; and support the goal of the Florida Heartland Rural Economic Development Initiative, Enterprise Florida, and the local and county comprehensive plans.

The goal of this project is to create an economically vibrant and diverse downtown business district; improve and revitalize downtown Wauchula; and increase commercial activity in Zolfo Springs and Bowling Green. It will achieve this by working in concert with other city initiatives and development plans by:

- Creating a framework for development – Key elements focus on enhancing community character, pedestrian friendliness, traffic circulation and housing options. The framework would also include guidelines for town/city gateways, facades and streetscapes, an inventory of heritage buildings/places, and opportunities to optimize land uses to attract businesses along the upgraded US 17 highway.
- Restore and renovate key heritage structures in Wauchula – Restoring, renovating and maintaining key heritage structures will improve their ability to withstand future disasters and will complement a revitalized downtown by attracting new businesses and customers.
- Redevelop key opportunity sites – In addition to the key heritage structures, many downtown spaces and buildings would benefit from a targeted approach to renovation and redevelopment and provide opportunities to fulfill the community's vision of a vibrant downtown.
- Create a downtown business and US 17 development / marketing plan – The plan will highlight the downtown and US 17 corridor area and result in a marketing brochure and targeted action plan that will highlight key themes, attractions, shops and restaurants to attract businesses and capture a portion of the tourism market in rural Florida.
- Encourage 2nd floor housing downtown – Utilizing existing downtown structures for housing will provide additional support for downtown businesses, additional sales tax revenue and help address the local housing shortage.

The cost of a sample renovation project (Wauchula train depot), marketing plan, survey of downtown buildings, development plan, and review/revision of local zoning ordinances is approximately $1.7 million.

Parks & Recreation
Laishley Park Improvements as Part of a Downtown Revitalization Strategy – Charlotte County, FL
Recovery Value: High

Charlotte County was left devastated by Hurricane Ivan, and the City of Punta Gorda, which had recently established itself as a thriving downtown of mom and pop shops, caught the brunt of the storm. Thus, the Long-Term Community Recovery plan included a comprehensive downtown revitalization element. This area is an important revenue generator to the county and city, and creates opportunities for intergovernmental coordination and public/private partnership.

Downtown revitalization cannot be accomplished with one or two projects. It requires a combination of key projects that form a comprehensive strategy for growth and renewal. The goal of the many projects included in this plan is to create an active and profitable downtown that is pedestrian friendly and that retains its unique characteristics. Laishley Park is one of a host of projects proposed for the renewal and reconstruction of Downtown Punta Gorda.

Laishley Park's location is not utilized to its fullest potential. Although the residents enjoy the park's open space, it can be developed as a focal point of downtown, with improvements such as landscaping, decorative lighting, a fountain and an open-air market. Improvements to Nesbit Street, including special paving, lighting, and streetscaping, will help it to serve as an entry to the park and waterfront area. The city is proposing a public building, which would contain restrooms, the harbormaster's office, and a restaurant. Consideration should be given to constructing a separate community center as a replacement for the damaged Bayfront Center. Relocating Bayfront to Laishley Park would draw additional visitors downtown. Each of these components works together to make a more attractive and functional downtown waterfront district.

The city's CRA has provided $1.45 million in funds out of the $5.2 million needed to fulfill the city's vision for Laishley Park.

Tourism

Develop a Peace River Heritage Corridor
Regional project for Southwest Florida
Recovery Value: High

Increased tourism within Southwest Florida, and specifically around the Peace River corridor in Hardee, DeSoto and Charlotte Counties, will foster economic growth and recovery from multiple hurricanes by stimulating new business and job opportunities. The goal of this project is to expand the existing economic development base of the three-county region by increasing regional tourism. It is consistent with the development plans and policies of the three counties and includes:

- Development of a Peace River Tourism Plan - Assess and define the unique identity of the Peace River Heritage Corridor.
- Formulation of a marketing strategy – Develop a targeted marketing campaign to attract tourists and receive their feedback and ideas for further regional improvements.
- Creation of a Peace River Heritage Corridor Brand - Create a unique identity that emphasizes the region's exceptional ecology, archeology, and recreational opportunities.

A number of development opportunities may jump-start the development of this corridor, including:

- Maximizing ecotourism / nature-based tourism – Acquire properties within the Peace River floodplain to extend existing recreational trails and provide further opportunities for walking, jogging, bird watching and biking. Other opportunities to increase ecotourism include the extension of state-designated canoe trails, improvement of 12 existing public boat/canoe launches and the increased marketing of freshwater and saltwater fishing opportunities.
- Maximizing agri-tourism and rural tourism – Establish a heritage agricultural tour to increase day trips within the three counties.

The cost of the tourism plan, marketing strategy and brand development, as well as one full-time staff person, is $535,000. The cost of carrying out the development opportunities is approximately $780,000.

APPENDIX III: Long-Term Community Recovery Project Template/Checklist

---

> The following questions should be addressed when developing a project for Long-Term Community Recovery. Information gathered and/or provided at the time of project development will assist in better definition of the project and will provide information needed in determining a project's recovery value.

Post-Disaster Community Need

1. Project Description: Provide general description of project to include location, cost (if known), funds currently available (if any), and other general characteristics of project.

2. Identify how project relates to damages from the disaster event.

3. Does project provide an opportunity to improve upon pre-disaster conditions? Explain.

4. Is project addressed in existing plans?

5. How does project related to key health and safety issues in the community?

6. Does the project leverage several potential sources of funding? What are they?

7. Document the community's support for the project.

8. Does the project benefit low to moderate-income households? To what extent?   Provide documentation or estimate.

9. Identify whether the project supports distinct social or cultural aspects of the community.

Project Feasibility

1. Identify and assess the probability of acquiring necessary funding within the project timeframe.

2. Assess compatibility of project with existing plans and regulations. Explain.

3. Make sure there are definable outcomes within the scope of the project.

4. Assess the feasibility of completing the project within an identified timeframe.

5. Identify whether the project has a champion or champions. Identify the champion(s).

Project Sustainability

1. Determine whether the project can pay for itself or be financed over the long-term without additional aid from local government. Provide estimates.

2. Identify whether the project or aspects of the project are identified in mitigation or safety plans for the area.

3. Does the project apply mitigation or safety measures to avert future losses? Explain.

4. Explain how the project addresses efficient land use strategies and/or supports principles of Smart Growth.

5. Explain geographic location of project within community and how it encourages connections to other nodes or activity centers within the community.

6. How does the project impact ecosystems within the community? Wildlife? Natural Areas? Air and Water Quality?

7. Estimate whether the project will result in reduction in water and/or energy use and whether it addresses innovative wastewater technologies.

8. Identify whether and how the project improves availability of mass transit or advances transportation solutions.

Economic Impact

1. Does the project replace pre-disaster jobs or provide new, permanent jobs?

2. Does the project rebuild or redevelop damaged properties using sustainable development measures?

3. Identify whether the project provides opportunities for affordable building space – purchase or lease.

4. Identify estimates of any increase in business income resulting from project.

5. Identify any new economic opportunities resulting from the project.
   a. Diversification of economy
   b. Job training/opportunities for increased wages
   c. Business attraction

6. To what extent does the project increase local capacity for economic development? Plans? New programs? Increases professional staff?

Project Visibility and Potential to Build Community Capacity

1. Identify whether the project has potential to obtain investment from a cross-section of community.

2. Document level of community awareness and recognition of project within the community.

3. Identify whether project addresses key services/operations in the community (city hall, water distribution, waste hauling, post office, etc.).

4. Does this project serve as a catalyst in attracting new development or other recovery projects?

5. Identify whether the project has the potential to attract various sources of financial support.

6. Document potential markets that could be impacted by the project; e.g., housing, retail, manufacturing, etc.

7. Identify the geographic area or areas that the project serves or supports.

8. Document any innovative techniques employed as part of the project.

9. Identify any new/improved public policy or principles that are a result of this project.

Project Linkages and Connections

1. Identify whether and how the project physically connects neighborhoods, key features within the community, districts, services, or communities and/or whether the project functions as a magnet to attract people from other parts of community.

2. Does the project support the existing resources of the community (cultural, physical, natural, or environmental)? Identify.

3. Document how project involved various local, state, or federal agencies/organizations as part of its planning, regulatory review, funding resources, etc.

4. Identify whether the project has an impact on the region; i.e., areas beyond the disaster-affected community.

5. Identify whether the project, or parts of the project, complement other projects and/or is part of an overall recovery/redevelopment strategy.

Quality of Life

1. Does the project promote existing strengths within the community? Existing tourism? Attract additional growth? Etc.

2. Identify whether project addresses community services, such as schools, libraries, cultural centers, community gathering places, recreational facilities, etc.

3. Identify whether the project affects critical facilities, such as hospital, fire and police stations, and other emergency response facilities.

4. Does the project enhance housing options and assisted living facilities?

5. Identify whether the project positively affects any culturally significant facilities or resources in the community.

This page intentionally blank.

A Guide to Determining Project Recovery Values

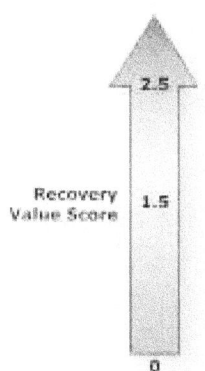

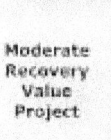

Recovery Value Score — 2.5, 1.5, 0

Community Interest Project

Low Recovery Value Project

Moderate Recovery Value Project

High Recovery Value Project

Recovery Value

HIGH
- Is a catalyst project with multiple impacts on the community
- Is directly related to damages
- Has community support and community-wide or regional benefits
- Is achievable and sustainable – has a champion
- Incorporates identified best practices for reducing future losses
- Creates economic opportunities
- Has a high visibility and builds community capacity
- Leverages and creates linkages to other projects and resources
- Enhances quality of life for the community

MODERATE
- Does not have community-wide or regional impacts
- Has limited community support and benefits
- Is difficult to achieve and sustain
- Has less definable outcomes
- Provides benefits for some economic sectors

LOW
- Has an indirect link to the disaster and its damages
- Has minimal community support or benefits
- Lacks the resources necessary for implementation
- Is difficult to achieve or sustain

COMMUNITY INTEREST
- May have significant public support
- May not produce results within 3-5 year recovery timeline
- Has little, if any, relationship to the disaster
- Does not produce identifiable benefits that promote recovery

www.ingramcontent.com/pod-product-compliance
Lightning Source LLC
Chambersburg PA
CBHW080540290526
45790CB00006B/2490